DANCE BOOK

When I take a breath and start to move, I construct a sentence. It is what happens when I exhale. A 'sentence' is logical, it has integrity and consistency. It does something. – Lee Connor, Dancer

larry goodell

2023

a compilation of poems about dance
poems used in collaboration with dancers
dancers I have worked with
have known & loved

pictures and memorabilia
dedicated to the memory of Lee Connor
1947-1987

cover photo of larry goodell & licea perea
rehearsing for tribute performance
for lee connor

thanks to Dr. David Bennahum
for his poem

Several of these poems first appeared
in *Firecracker Soup,* Cinco Puntos Press 1990

 I am grateful for the wonderful dance photographs
from the collections
of Lorn MacDougal
and the late Lee Connor

a duende press
celebration
2023
placitas, new mexico

DANCE BOOK

danzantes

a contemporary dance company

kimo theatre
april 8 &9, 1983
8:OO pm

a contemporary dance company

james a. little theatre
june 3, 1983
8:15 pm

Sunday Morning, April 10, 1983

Connor Makes Humorous, Welcome Return With Danzantes

His humor and regard for his partners, whether only organized modern dance company now per-

Ms. Paras accompanied Connor in the premiere of separate ways in a satire on sexual mores and op-

By PAMELA SALMON
Journal Feature Writer

POEMS BY LARRY GOODELL

1   **Boogie On the Square /1987

2   The Dance /1977

3   Lorn /Feb 1979

6   Lee /3 Feb 1979

7   Her Clown Dance Home /28 Jun 1978

8   The House Between the Words /14 Sep 1977

10   The Only Dance There Is /Apr 1980

14   Dance And /1981

18   **Reagan Is /1986

20   Pegasus of Love /26 Jul 1981

22   **Video Shmideo /1982

24   **Kiss It Right /1982

29   Dance Stanza /15 Feb 1983

36   **Fashionism, /Mar 1983

39   Mirrors /7 Jan 1984

42   **Common Sense Stanza /1983

44   A Letter from Durham /1984

45   *Voices /30 Oct 1984

51   *The Written Work /25 Oct 1984

52   *Manner /8 Mar 1984

57   *A Dance Again /4 Feb 1985

58   *Solar Arcane Boogie Woogie /15 Dec 1985

62   Keats Going By /Sep - 13 Oct 1987

64   Garden Art /29 & 30 Jan 1988

67   Dance Art, for Arthur Armijo /1994

72   It's All Over, Bub, /12 Nov 83, Afterthought /20 Feb 2015

74   He Who Pays The Piper Calls The Tune - Lee Connor

82   For Lee Connor - Dr. David Bennahum

83   Richard Thompson items

84   Sun In The Mountain (About, and Poem) /18 Dec 1977

"Words" performed in Santa Fe 14 Jan 1979
all marked poems were performed in collaborations
*Voices, Manner, Solar Arcane Boogie Woogie, A Dance Again,
The Written Work* performed as part of "The Seeing-Is-Believing"
program, June 1985.
**In collaboration with Danzantes, Lee Connor solo, or Licea Perea solo.

Note: Licia Perea did a reconstruction of *Solar Arcane Boogie Woogie,*
and George Kennison a reconstruction of *Written Work.*

Took tap dance, yes, one of the few boys, in Roswell, New Mexico, McEvoy School of Allied Arts, but never, not ever a dancer (except wild amateur nights at the Thunderbird Bar in Placitas). Thank you dear Zelma McEvoy for teaching piano and dance and organizing those big performances.

Lee Connor - Path With Heart - photo by Lawrence Licht

BOOGIE ON THE SQUARE

The light that is the fair, the light that is the fair
We boogie on the square, we boogie on the square
And know no one is soon, and know no one is soon
And know no one is far, as far as Zanzibar
But here and now and nimble, quick and ordinary
Depending on how you look at anything, if you look
If you look like a canary or
If you look like yourself, or
If you look *and* don't look, like
Anything or anyone or any look looks like—
Boogie on the square and move everywhere
Be little and big, customary and aware
The light is fair and travels in and out and
Picks up the board like a carpet anywhere, an - y - where.

/from *Here On Earth* (La Alameda Press)

1

THE DANCE

Pirouette in the substance of nothing
and what do you get?

Fireworks in the substance of nothing
how do they work?

Oxygen, a tourniquet on each firework
a tourniquet on each dancer.

Hold the dancers down and do not let them dance,
and what do you get?

The dance.
The Dance with a capital D.

The D Dance.
Dance for D's.

D D Day
when they all went home to pray.

Pray to their Susies and sisters.
The ones with the name stay the same.

And therefore they are sane.

LORN

Grace, ultimately
a race
to the finish.

Amaryllis blooming buoyantly.

Lorn MacDougal - Spanish Dance

Lee Connor - Photograph by Lawrence Licht

LEE

Your head in spirals
gonads   go
leap   caught
form

is the merry extension
of content –
rocked heart low.

/3Feb79

Path With Heart - Photograph by Lawrence Licht

HER CLOWN DANCE HOME

/for Lee & Lorn 28Jun78

He
haw
      ho
   he
haw
      ho

————————

   home
      oh

————————

   haw
      home

————————

   him
haw
      home

————————

   her
      him home

————————

   he
haw

   ho
   stress, confess, bless

————————

   him
her
      home

————————

oh
   him her home.

————————

   He
haw
      ho
      ho!

THE HOUSE BETWEEN THE WORDS

for Lee Connor & Lorn MacDougal & their
orchard house beginning

Ground broken breaking   front loader trench making
ditch-digging foundation cement pouring water runs like
pebbles slick as mud soft to harden gray, the slates
all the grays to harden white slate foundation where the
walls like ancient Turkish mosques transplanted to the orchard
grow faster than the trees man-made up.

Blessings come from nowhere and are everywhere
as slow moving as the mushroom quick to appear.
Blessings come from the North the South the Easy West.
You come from the East, the Above the Below in your dance.

A dance is a leap a glide a slide with music or without,
weaving, a line, breaking, forming, down under up below burrowing
sitting there on glass, sliding through the tunnel of vision
burst out a flower, a gonad, the sun the moon a chrysalis.

Ugly smiling clasping throwing mimicking and panting,
prowess in the leap the movement on and off, a panther
snake, bird, hippopotamus.
                                An ode to the dance, watch out
the dance a man and woman special in the air on the floor
all in white or naked nothing   special as the talent that
becomes grace, ever the thousand studies, exercises,
stretching, yoga on point.

Lee the fire balances on the butt and turns over
slaps the floor leaps
the nose slices through the air of the stage
buffoons clowns pantaloons tights, no one on stage
the dancing continues.

8

What is yours is yours, dancing round the trees
peaches falling on your feet, Lorn enters sits down turns
cavorts, nitpicks in the air, looks wild and is wild
gets up on a woman and balances there
dances through the primary colors to the apple trees
pear trees in a circle, plum bushes in a line,
        dancers in a straight line
in a circle broken, come under hand to hand Lee and Lorn,
have no words to describe the beauty of a Tiffany lamp.

You glow on the stage of this orchard in this house here.
House or Dance, no one knows the origin.
A Home is a place, the Village here.

Take care with your luck, and blessings come from everywhere,
even the chamisa you cut blossoms yellow now
here in September where the waltzing out-in cat-dance
pony-dance on-edge dance celebrates celebrate dance,
dance studio basic to the space that is your body dances under
to the side and over you, holds you and us in total freedom of your
great dancer talents.

I give you one I give you all let's have a ball, formal or free.
It all goes into your blessing like airs, glittering host and hostess
dancing up the stairways to the bedroom above.
Let the design be the grace that is the delicate tension
we live between hold us like tightrope, a level on a string
coming in from Bob the builder and his friends Bruce and John and
whoever else lends the hand. Jamie, all of us, let us all be blessed.

/14Sep77
Amazing to have 2 wonderful dancers for our new neighbors.

9

& Thanks to Lee Connor
for his Dance
Catch As Catch Can.

THE ONLY DANCE THERE IS

We opened his heart and out fell art.
We opened the art. *It* had a heart.
We opened the heart of his art–
      Out
    Fell
A dart.
We threw the dart and hit a bell
The dart broke and out fell
A little rolled-up diagram
Of the path to his heart—
From the toes to the brain and out
Into the air and back again.

We followed the diagram
And came back to the hollow
Where his heart had been.

A hummingbird was hovering there!
We caught it, it fought
We let it go, it flew wild
Into a window, fell, died
Quivering on the ground.
We opened up the mouth of the bird
And there was the poet's soul—
Pure song, mercury quivering
Hot silver shimmering in our hands
It fell from our fingers to the ground
And disappeared.

        Slowly
Up grew a standard tree forty feet or more.
And in the center of that American Elm
There was a hollow
        And in the hollow
There was a singing that didn't stop
Singing to you and me,
A muted continuing song that pleases
Eases the morning along and abruptly
Stops in the evening to our hearing
Singing beyond our ear's range.

We took it out in our hands
Trying to understand it.
It beat against our fingers, invisible
And floated off into the air
A deep drumming under it
    Supporting it like legs as
    It returned to the tree
    And took up beating in the hollow.

    All the leaves of the Elm had fallen to the ground
    As winter ceased to hear
    The beating singing in the hollow.
    We took the singing out again
    And put it back into the center
    Of the hollow where his heart had been.

The drumming and the singing grew
More visible and formed the outer
Shell of his heart.
The inner heart started beating
To the sound of the drums
As the stage behind him
Turned a light blue and
The dancers came out singing old
English rounds as they danced.

The light grew behind them
As they criss-crossed dancing
Holding hands and then running
Closing, breaking, disappearing
Singing rounds dying out
As another started up
And all took up the round the sound was
The singing in the center
Of the heart in my chest
As I sat and watched the blue light
Fade out on the stage.

And the dancers catch as catch can
Throwing voices back and forth
Turning in their rounds
Sing and reel, and fade away
In my ears' inner turning
Sitting with my heart beating
To their disappearing dance
Quiet, away—
Sitting with something left
Singing inside my chest.

/April 1980

Lee Connor

DANCE AND

for Lee Connor

                              The dance
                           the dance
                        ants in the pants
                     uncles in his carbuncles
                    dance no trance
                  just ordinary dance
                extraordinary dance
            your common most dance
        the kind that gets you
              up to dance
              can't keep your feet
                    from stomping toes
                    from tapping just
                        a plain old dance
                      the music stops
                  you keep on dancing
                  ants in your pants
              you dance your dance
              your heart keeps pumping
        dance and turn
        you can't control
    you're onto soul
    you're in the running
        light and sunning
            dark and quick
                jack be quick
                    nimble and sure
                        sway and pure
                          say and tour

dash and trash
stash and flee
cut corners jerk
and tumble turn
squeak and back turn
flip turn honest
rip air clip air sweep air up and throw
around the eyes sweep the thrown out   draw back
turn in come in home in *close* in touch in
stop and turn
dance the hand the fingers burn
the heart floats out you catch it back
you got them all up out of their chairs
they're looking following hearts beat faster
after you   one step behind
the dance that finds
the trick in hand the snap in turns
the swallowed up and spit out line
the sailing slow sure landing
what was land arroyos calm-
touch down the stream rushes on.

/1981, in *Firecracker Soup*, (Cinco Puntos Press)

HOMAGE

A program
of Bach harpsichord music
accompanied by
specially created new dances

Rodey Theatre
in UNM's Fine Arts Center

Friday and Saturday
February 13-14, at 8 p.m.

Harpsichordist Susan Patrick

Choreography by Lee Connor

For reservations contact
the UNM Fine Arts Box Office
277-4402

1981(?)

16

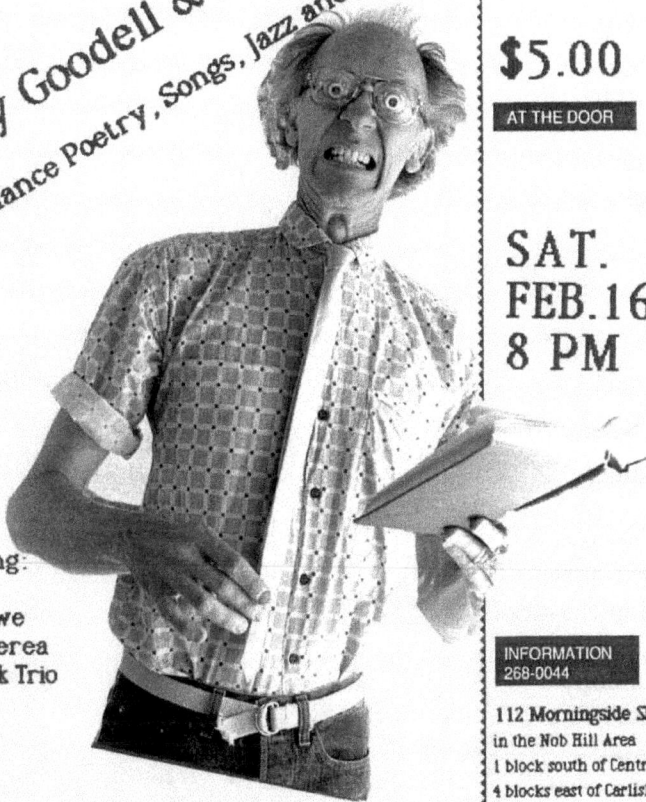

outpost productions presents

Larry Goodell & Friends

Performance Poetry, Songs, Jazz and Dance

$5.00
AT THE DOOR

SAT.
FEB.16
8 PM

featuring:

Zimbabwe
Alicia Perea
Guralnick Trio

INFORMATION
268-0044

112 Morningside SE
in the Nob Hill Area
1 block south of Central
4 blocks east of Carlisle

THE OUTPOST
PERFORMANCE SPACE

Collaborations with (A)licia Perea - "Pegasus of Love" & "Reagan Is"

REAGAN IS

a dildo
a doorstop
a drip
a dungeon
a dodo
a deacon
a dunce
a dilly
a dork
a dupe
a dink
a dick
a dong
a drudge
a dingaling
a dolt
a dimmer switch
a dime-a-dozen
a dyed-in-the-wool
a dirigible
a dinkaroony
a deflatable
a demented
a decomposed
a doom-a-flitchy
a demagnetized
a desensitized
a discombobulated
a disimpaired

a disestablished
a disinclined
a detour
a disattached
a doorbell
a decal
a decoy
a dumb-dumb
a doomsday
a dilleybob
a defecation
a deed
a dude
a dung
a dickeybird
a donkey-doo
a diddle-ee-poop
a dunk-ee-dorey
a dollie-dunker
a dispatched
a derelict
a dud
a dip
a din
a dad
a dead
a did
a done.

/from *Firecracker Soup* (Cinco Puntos Press),
Licia Perea created a dance to this, a poem often repeated . . .

PEGASUS OF LOVE

Love goes riding out of the cellar into the attic
on wings of love
goes out the attic window with the hot air
comes right down into some spaghetti twist
on the fork be*fore* I eat it
*aft*er I eat it
that popular new dance - the macaroni jerk
the lasagne lisp
the manicotti drag
the vermicelli chase
dancing is love eating itself up
you are what you eat if you dance a lot
on wings of soup
on horseradish
on horse's wings

       Oh fabled and mirrored Pegasus
       Winged Horse of Poetry
       Flying into the large salon mirror
       and out again
       There are two winged Pegasuses
       one for each side of the brain
one is real, the other mirrored, fabled, half-seen

       Mirror mirror on the wall
       let us love once and for all
       protected and assured
       my wife and I my lover līve
       my lover līve protected all
       love has wings up out from the head up
       out from the body love
       sets us dancing sets us free
       before the final black curtain of stars falls.

/26Jul81
Licia Perea, dance

Talking to Licia Perea, Jennifer Predock and others
at Connor Tribute rehearsal - photographs by Lenore Goodell

After Seeing Licea Perea in *A Slumber of Reason*, based on Goya's *Los Caprichos* rather recently at the Hispanic Cultural Center in Albuquerque . . . I wrote . . .

dance, singing, masks, film, acting, like an opera but always coming back to dance, dancers speaking, singing, Goya's magnificent Los Caprichos etchings swirling, floating from the huge background screen, Madrid becoming the burning of Baghdad, the Inquisition becoming questioning of an "illegal alien" with devilish and comic overtones . . . Licia Perea at the top of her form, the music interweaving the whole panorama of our time Goya's time together. BRAVO! Jose Garcia Davis and all . . .

VIDEO SHMIDEO

video
shmideo
pideo
crit-eo
spit-eo
snit-eo
skit-eo
stit-eo
fit-eo
smitteo
flit-eo
grit-eo
kideo
bid-eo
did-eo
gid-eo
knit-eo
tit-eo
pit-eo
video

city-o
kit-eo
hit-eo
grit-eo
lid-eo
zid-eo
video
tit-eo
spit-eo
shit-eo
video
grit-eo
kitty-o
jit-eo
pip-eo
flip-eo
nip-eo
crip-eo
gig-eo
rig-eo
jig-eo
kig-eo

```
  snip-eo
tip-eo
  sit-eo
tetty-o
  pig-eo
gip-eo
  sis-eo                              flib-eo
piss-eo                              fibeo
  fiss-eo                            fab-eo
tiffeo                               fie-beo
  biffeo                             fabio
riffeo                               vib-eo
  snaffio                            vab-eo
baffio                               vibe-eo
  taffy-o                            vabe-eo
video                                vie-deo
  shnitty-o                          video
pity-o                               vade-eo
  video                              vee-deo
libby-o                              vo-deo
  crib-eo                            vay-deo
ditty-o                              vi-de-o.
  video
shmib-eo
```

collaboration
Connor '82

KISS IT RIGHT

Photograph by Greg Johnston

Don't cry
and die
just lie
and tie
a fly
to the sky
and sigh
a guy
that's high
and buy
a pie
try
my
ride

glide
hide
the tide
subsides
and guides
you cry
don't lie
try
to kiss
the light
and twist
your life
a bit
more bite
light as
a kite
kiss
that's right
you hold
on tight
and kiss
your life
don't miss
the height
we just
are here
and must
be tight
just you
and I
and this
whole night
just you
and I
and this
whole night

We must
be tight
just you
and I
and kiss
we just
are here
and this
whole night
not miss
the height
we must
be here
and kiss
the night
just you
and I
and we
are tight
not miss
the ride
not miss
the sight
no risk
no lie
no miss
a try
no cry
no hitch
just you
and I
to fly
the sky
and glide
and ride

be here
and kiss
we just
don't miss
cant miss
we lift
the rift
the tiff
we shift
and give
the gift
we shift
and hold
on tight
the kiss
we must
be right
we're here
we must
be tight
not miss
the night
we just
are here
and kiss
it right.

/14oct82

Lee Connor choreographed
and performed dance to "Kiss It Right."

Almond tree planted in memory of Lee Connor in back of Connor and Macdougal studio in Placitas, photo by Cirrelda Snyder Bryan 2022

DANCE STANZA

*B*ody poise
hands fingers toes
dancing
relations
    whenever I turn
I've been someplace
someplace   ha *ha*
ha *ha*   someplace
 ser I ous ly
hands fingers toes
   an electric
displacement
   a kind overall
aura
    bone joint
aura
orally
body
    aurally yours
to rest
but for words
words for butts
bats on birds
birds on nests
trees on skies
skies on hills
hills on the best
best on best
best on rainbows, dirty
rainbows
   washing

weather
   after
snowstorm
mud
and ruts

Connor, Perea and Marina Baden
Photo: Kim Jew

Village
growing
    people
learning
    jobbing
driving
    coming
home to
    higher
madness
    where it's
close
    so close
to sane
    Placi-
ditas
    higher
same old
thing
    the rich
and bold
    take over
all
    the weak and
talented
    bite their
stars
    sleep all
night
    get up
dance
    the working

preparation

working
    your body

over clouds that
    come down
    like

friendly fog
the winter breaks
your heart aches less
    and less

the prison
    of
the days
    and nights' unending
    spiral
breaks

crocus rows
on rows and rows of odd spaced
bulbs
    bumping
skyband
    lowered
fog and
    waiting
garden
    oh the
spring
    before
the spring
    the pre-spring
    prelude
    dawn
    a-toking
    or
    a-teaing
    oh just getting up at dawn
    the pre-dawn
    held
    ever
    lasting
    in your palm
    the right palm
    or is it left it
    came up out of –

I dance to accompany my vision
up and out of my mouth
as poet singing many singings
words of earflap –
staccato pizzicato
stigmato boiled potato
up and out of my working mind
I dance   accompany
my vision
out my working
mind
    the body out

excelsior
    used
to be the
packing

      now it's styrofoam to roam
      the country like
      bloated horses died of flies
         our carefully protected
      humanity
      that all too often
      would get blown to hell

      our moral
      surprise

            dancers
and the *artists* on the edge
of each ridge touching
as the blue sky soars in obvious
disattachment
to these hills the Montezuma
ridge striated jagged pancake levels
stacked and singing in the only
decent sky song returning

of new high words *New*
Mexico that all flatlands hope
and pray they'll become

love when there's more than elbow room
to breathe
our dance in walking aerobic becoming
right out where we
ought to live

ten years longer

when we live
here where the time's only warp
that's left us is   giant
Americans besieged by rival giants now
we hoped and helped
to create
welcome what it's
all about
competition with a moral
aim
the spring
busts out
to follow hymning new
nuevo pagan joy songs
that have the care moderation of
the wild true spirit in
the two of us

        scilla   blue
        daffodil   pendant white
        tulip   *scar*let edged yellow
        daffodil   small vivid orange cup with white perianth
        tulip a terra-cotta orange
        snow crocus -
        soft lemon-yellow-shaded lavender
           very early

extra early tulip Tarda
        yellow and white star shape
      lily   black-dragon strain
      white-white   with outside a rich purple-brown
     and don't forget the winter aconite
    little early low yellows

   up these muscles we
    meet again
     across the borders
     the great dropping fences
    what all the struggle
   is all about
   I wish I knew as
    the world regroups
   as earth
   the world regroups
  as Earth
maybe

    /15Feb83

DANZANTES, Inc.
The seeing-is-believing wishful-thinking follies
featuring
LEE CONNOR solo dance
Larry Goodell, poet
Jeffrey Stolet, piano
collaborations:
Barbara Bock, Jim Linnell,
Jennifer Predock-Linnell
June 19 & 20   KiMo Theatre
8:00 pm   Tickets: $6 adult, - 4 sen./stu.

TAKING RISKS;
CREATING CONTROVERSY

1987 Lecture Series

Performing/Performance Art: *Hot or Not?*	*Taking Risks with* *New and Emerging Artists*
Wednesday, April 22	Thursday, May 28
7:30 p.m.	7:30 p.m.
Albuquerque Museum	Albuquerque Museum
2000 Mountain Road NW	2000 Mountain Road NW
Featuring	*Featuring*
Lee Connor, Dancer, Danzantes, UNM Dance Faculty	**Fay Abrams** Mariposa Gallery, Albuquerque
Larry Goodell, Poet	**Linda Durham**
Martha Trolin, Performance Artist Coordinator, 500 2nd Street performance space	Linda Durham Gallery, Santa Fe **Kris Kron** Kron-Reck Gallery, Albuquerque
Moderator: Barbara Grothus, Artist President AUA Board of Directors	*Moderator:* Cheryl McLean, Artist Member AUA Board of Directors

Tickets at the Door: $2 general/$1 AUA members
Watch for Future Announcements

FASHIONISM

Fashionism
fish in setting
fish in netting
fish in fashion
fission-ism
fashion's ism
fascist fashion
fast in fashion
in fascistic
face in fashion
fashion fascist
fast-ass fashion
fashion feeding
thin-ass fashion
starving fashion
Auschwitz fashion
flashin bones
and joints in fashion

fish in fashion
bone fish fashion
fish and fox in
gaunt lip fashion
gauntlet fascist
fascist face in
feces fashion.
feces fascist
face lift fashion
faceless face lift
fishless fashion
face in fish out
faceless fashion
flashin fashion
Russian fashion
fusion fission
fission fusion
fission fusion.

fusion fashion
photo flashin
fissionistic
fashionistic
phase in shit stick
stick in fashion
shit stick fashion
fashion fusion fission fluxion
faction flack shun shoes in fashion
fascist fraction fractured fashion
flash in fractured photo friction
fish in photo fractured fashion
-istic, pristic, cystic, shistic
glyph and gloat remote bag fashion
bag your boots and kick out fashion
fascist female fasting he-males
thin bone aching starving fashion
ritzy titsy gargoyle bean pole
rag pole gag hole bean pole fashion
take your boots off kick out fashion
butts on bean poles. tight-laced ache holes
sex-exploited hate-kick fashion
fish and nets and future fashion
people fast in future fashion
future fashion people future
people as they are in fashion
fashion as a person's person
as they are is what's in fashion
people in the future
people as they are in fashion
take your shoes off kick out fashion
as it was no longer fashion
fascist female hatred fashion
people as they are are fashion
people here and there are fashion
future fashion is no fashion
people as they are in fashion.

/Mar 1983 Collaboration with Danzantes Dance Group

Under It - phenomenal and prophetic dance -
Lee and Lorn - photo by Cathy Wanek

a poet and a dancer in performance
at the Kimo Theater
in Albuquerque - Larry and Lee https://youtu.be/siofaHIxXbE

MIRRORS

1.

Seeing myself in others' mirrors
is always robbing them of my visions.
What I see in their places is partially mine.
Partially mine as when I see in my mirrors.
We have one in the bathroom two foot square
and I use a rearview mirror Larry Massingale gave me,
the other Larry from Roswell, gave me a rearview mirror
that I use to clip my hair, to see in back.

We should have more mirrors in this house.

Joel has a round rearview mirror I've used recently.
It's handy but it doesn't have a handle
like Larry's.
To look at something reversed
is crazy
but that's all I've ever seen of myself.
Could I look really different right side out?
With my face toward the sun ?

Seeing myself in others' mirrors is like
wallowing in their depths.
Or shallow vertical glass ways.
"You cannot touch me because I'm a
cold cross-product of you.
An illusion which is a reflection of reality.
A cold reminder to the warm.
A simply tantalizing way of thought."

It was once thought back in the 18th Century
that mirrors were the eyes of God –
mirrors are the images of the wives of god.
The Goddesses' husbands are in the back room
looking at themselves in the mirror.

There are ten of them with ten mirrors in ten rooms
all of them to one goddess–
although they think of goddesses
as many wives to themselves!
As if you had to have more women than men.

2.
The eyes are looking in on each other
during rarer moments.
As if you had to raise your eyes to see into some-
body's soul.
And notice there are no mirrors
when you do–
everything is the pleasure of communion
even if it is the end
of a business transaction
when the eyes meet
over the counter
change has been made
your eyes contact–
the most amazing thing about
business
has nothing whatsoever
to do with mirrors–
when stranger meets stranger
almost as friend.
An agreement of satisfaction.
If we all could meet before our parting ways
that way
the place would be a safer world.

Seeing myself
in others' faces.
Reflections in the glasses
or eyes
in the mirrors that aren't mirrors–
reflections of themselves,
is not what I see every day

when I shave
wet-brush my hair
wash my teeth
wash my hands
wash the new Sequoia Kohler basin
keeping it shiny
and seeing ourselves
in it.

3.
The end of that fumble was a long pass
and a goal was thrown–
shake up everybody
by what you say
what you sing
popular one.
Who won the game?
The teams were mirror images
of themselves
and they played until no one won.
They were a real Sunday football team.
They took off their clothes
and agreed to play in the nude
and not hit each other
so hard.
That was the business agreement
on a national scale
that we all hoped
and yearned for
while it was going on
all over the world.

/7Jan84, Collaboration

COMMON SENSE STANZA

There's nothing as common as common sense
or as nonsensical
    Where has it gotten us?
right at the core of where we are,
nonsensical –
    like wars,
    the pressure of population.
Common sense will get you out of anything–
*fan*tasy is common sense
    without fantasy
you cannot *fo*cus
    fantasy is pe*ri*pheral
    threatening to take   over   focus.
Common sense drives
fantasy out
and returns to a more ma*ture*
way of dealing with things
which is different than
the way your neighbor
deals with things
but common sense *sounds* good in the air
    a generality
    we can all accept
a general way to deal with particulars
that sounds right
    and yet another *na*tion may not say so
thus common sense *is*
fantasy –
yet changing and differing,
the same thing referring to itself
as the god almighty
in a little man's way of
doing things –
it's common sense!
    any idget
would know so
    any idget
would *say* so:

there's nothing as common
as common sense.

Without a border
there is no picture
    without a sideline
there is no mainline
    without a left right-up-and-down
there is no *forward*
    without a *back*ward(↑)
there is no forward
    without exhaustion
there is no center
    without walking around
there is no standing still
    without constant mo*bili*ty
there is no *rest*
    without something *out there*
there isn't something
in here:
1983 is the *year* of common sense
    a little bird told me
    if we don't use it
we won't have it
    nonsensical
common sense.(↓)
You hit the *nail* on the head.
The pen is mightier than the sword–
    a pencil too.
Common sense is a roundtable with a hole in it
    a large *do*nut size hole
you project your agreement in there–
    after the meeting it was said
"We used our common sense
which we the leaders never have:
we got it from the people we used to be –
everyone else   has common sense.
We borrowed it   from you
and thus we won't have war
thank you –
it-*must*-be-common *sense.*"

                      /1983 Collaboration

FROM A LETTER

to Lenore and Larry from Lee Connor in North Carolina, 1984

[handwritten letter reproduction]

   . . .

My classes are, in fact, going very well. People are particularly excited about my Improvisation class, and I turned a whole slew of the dance educators on to the fantastic possibilities for applying Laban's Space Harmony concepts to creating movement patterns in teaching. So I have the gratification of feeling that I am adding awareness of some movement awarenesses to American modern dance that are not otherwise much considered here, and that feels good. Just plain good to come out of the boondocks, and sense I can make an impact.

On July 17th I'm going to perform 'Strand' (Stravinsky) on the Faculty concert. I wish Larry were here so we could do the poems. People would think that was pretty wonderful, I think. Oh, well . . . another time, maybe.

College Station, Durham NC

Love, Lee

VOICES . . .

Always there was an unbending repetition which threatened
        to enslave him.
What must he do,
            warp the voices, try to throw them out?
            force them into some socially acceptable behavior?
            kill plurality,
            simplify
            hear only one
            and deny it, its strength from beyond, tie it down
            nail it down to a 2 by 4?
            to a block of wood he used to burn in the stove
            for warmth?

If only there was some clear use
that would not repeat itself.

What value is something nobody else hears?

            Is he some pint-sized Joan of Arc
            but without God over her shoulder

an insane man being whipped and thrown around
in an exclusive way.

Simply change,   turn over a new leaf, be of some use to his family.
Put all this mystery into clarity,
the transmogrified voice.

An utterance of speech that might take place over some one's
coffeetable
            or better yet
someone's desk,
a business transaction
            then
turned to pleasure
that became a firm bank account
a refined script on TV 7

an announcement of a shift in life
that everyone can understand

          what is it
what *is* it?
          Always
there was an unbending repetition which threatened to enslave him
and did
     . . . A G A I N
unless he said *no,* simply let it drift by
          that's it –
          if he only had the heart
to constantly say goodbye
let it drift by like an ordinary person
who never hears such things
or thing –

not to hear it
          or when he did
let it trail by
the life of a poet he could hear
almost touching him as it came near
and he didn't remember it
          certainly didn't write it down -

          but whose life was that
          when he heard it
          pass by?

And now forgotten?
          Whose voices were they
got on a train and left.

The train pulled away and refused to stay.

A train of voices
of some lives of poets
got off and brushed through him
activating his ears
every now and then
then left.

Who were
they that never seemed to do him any good
but a little local laughter
where oddity was liked.
In some small circles.

Who were they
leaving him again
after doing the same thing again
        with variations endlessly
calling.
        That made his life
one of them
although there was no apparent connection.

And would someday take him off with them
for good,
or so he imagined.

He imagined everything and complained.
        obsessed and rare
useless and warped

weird

until it was over
and it left him crazy

he couldn't get rid of
        secretly
fascinated.

        What

and why?

        When?
Why him?

/30Oct84 Collaboration

47

Wonderful Lorn MacDougal, Lee Connor dancing
"It's Either a Feast . . . "

"It's either a feast . . . "

Arthur Armijo & Jennifer Predock - reconstruction of "It's Either a Feast
. . ." for the Connor Tribute. Photos by Lenore Goodell.

Picnic basket of stuffed fruit created by Lenore Goodell
for "It's Either a Feast . . ."

THE WRITTEN WORK

I *want* to write until everything *about* it is written. If it's written out I *know I wrote it* because I write it until there isn't *any*thing more to write about the *subject.* That is, I exhaust exhaustion. I terminate termination. I'm so *big* that I exhaust things. I pester them to death to get the pearls out of swine, the oyster out of the *shell.* I just generally rub the hell out of it till it comes and is sore. Writing is something to tackle every day in every way and there's *always more.* What's frustrating is that I'll have to die before I can write everything I want to write. As a matter of fact there's *nothing* I don't *want* to write. I *must* write *everything* until I die. And then, probably, I'll go on writing. I'll have to write *forever* if I'm going to get to writing everything in *all* the *ways* I *want* to *write.* Writing about it *once* isn't enough. You have to come back over it again but this time hitting all the things you missed until finally you've got it all. That's the only way I can write and if I don't write there's nothing left worth doing. Certainly nothing worth living. Writing is the worth of life when life seems immaterial. Writing is the spirit *and* the worth. Without writing there is *nothing* but the avoidance of it. And without writing, *there could not be me.* I am writing everything there is about it, and there is no end to what anyone will ever *say* about what I write and how I say so much about anything there is to say and how I say it any way anybody ever thought of before or after, because I don't in*tend* to stop writing when I've got to write everything there is to say before I'm *through* and when I'm through there won't be any *need* for anyone anywhere to *bother* writing anything again *about* anything or *from* anything or *because* of anything because *I* will have *amassed* the *writing* of it somewhere in my collected works which *of course will be definitive.*

/Collaboration, Lee and me

51

MANNER

The miser
the mister
the master
the masher

the man
the moan
the main
the mine

the most
the must
the mast
the mass

the muscle
the hustle
the hassle
the missile

the mess
the miss
the mouse
the muss

the hate
the hit
the heat
the hack

the rack
the rake
the rape
the rat

the wretch
the reach
the wrench
the ranch

the business
the bastard
the beefer
the lizard

the gizzard
the gazer
the gasser
the guzzler

the pounder
the hounder
the hitter
the hunter

the hater
the rater
the rudder
the rotter

the got her
the goat
the goad
the god

the rod
the road
the raid
the rude

the prude
the prod
the dude
the hood

the fuss
the face
the false
the fast

the one
the man
the hun
the hand

the arm
the aim
the owner
the armor

the heavy
the lover
the loner
the boner

the baller
the banger
the bender
the biter

the fighter
the fatter
the fitter
the madder

the rougher
the bigger
the tougher
the hitter

the calm
the cold
the caged
the bold

the bod
the good
the bad
the bud

the crazy
the brassy
the brazen
the brash

the boss
the brains
the brawn
the blood

the mister
the master
the molder
the masher

the man
the one
the calm
the gun

the grin
the groan
the groin
the grind

the great
the grown
the grouch
the slouch

the one
and only
lifer
lonely

lover
blunder
softer
under.

/8Nov1984 Lee and me

Collaborative poster to benefit New Mexico Aids Services Photo Bob Vocca,
poster design Lenore Goodell

DANCE AGAIN

/for Lee Connor & the Danzantes

We danced we did
we danced the did did dance
the dance we did dance in we did
we did the dance indeed we did
the did and done and dead with dance
the dance done in, we did it in
we did it in the dance we did
the did did dance and done we did
the dance again and did the whole thing in
we did it in we did the dance
and did it in we danced it dead
    until it twisted
danced and did it back again
we danced it in and did it in
and brought it back to dance again
we brought it in and danced a sin until it sings
we danced it in and out again
and did we dance? did we dance?
did we dance it in again?
until it sings until it sung
until the song sang again
we danced a din and danced a sing
song again we did a dance
and danced we did
we did a dance a dance we did
again we did a dance again
again we didn't dance again
we stopped and didn't dance the dance
was done we did it dance and all
the ball was over dance and hall
we did a dance once and for all
we did a did and done dance and did
the dance we did again.
And did we dance again
and did we dance again.

/4Feb85 - Collaboration

SOLAR ARCANE BOOGIE WOOGIE

Solar arcane boogie woogie
nookie cookie ragwell rookie
cocaine cocky cutie cootie
bagwell bogwell buggy Bogie

baggy boogie waggy woogie
molar octane buggy cutie
nutty rookie highkey goody
gumbo gummy gitchy goomie

whole earth octave real key boogie
baggy cutworm Katie cutie
rugby ruddy batty buddy
solar octane daddy duty

ruddy rootie tootie snooty
buddy rocky ratty rooty
booty hooty rockwell gummy
half-earth octane ugly scummy

solar molar boogie woogie
bagwell bogwell buggy goodie
whole earth octane solar gloomy
pick up getchur boogie woogie

waggy get up active nookie
cracky cookie hacky hookie
a cook and a snappy heart-warm happy
booky plunky baggy boogie

waggy woogie arcane cutie
whole earth octane wackie rookie
nutty nookie sidekick buddy
molar popped in poppy pucky

rockwell raggy baggy booty
solar octane boogie woogie
whole earth octave double duty
round your corners rocky cutie

rubber rooty rattled cootie
solar octet lunar moony
boogie woogie catchy toonie
ancient rune boggy dune

molar cockaigne boogie woogie
cocky cocktail talky cutie
walk in waggy rock out boogie
baggy eat your nutty cookie

snap your fingers rooty tooty
solar arcane boogie woogie.

/15Dec1985 Collaboration

Video of reconstruction of this dance choreographed
by Lee Connor danced by Licea Perea at the Connor Tribute:
https://youtu.be/UqkHtI8wXzg

59

Danzantes presents

we danced we did

a tribute to Lee Connor
and
benefit for New Mexico Aids Services

KiMo January 29 and 30

Information: 277-1855

Reserved Seating

Tickets from Giant Ticketmaster
  or at the door
  2 for $25 or
$15 centre orchestra & mezzanine
$10 sides & balcony (student discount)

Arthur Armijo
Eva Encinas
Larry Goodell
George Kennison
Lorn MacDougal
Alicia Perea
and
Geoffrey Budd Landis·painter
KiMo Gallery Jan.13-Feb.15

Lee Connor

Lee told me that seeing "The Green Table"
a twentieth century dance masterpiece
by Kurt Jooss (1932) turned him to give his
life to dance.

KEATS GOING BY

for Lee, a very literate man . . .

Death goes defying trance leaps–
that is the open and the closed.

Oh Death, dead as Thou art

having grasped Lee
take him gently to Paradise
having long suffered the wreck and recoil
of disease

or the maidens that we all are
lifting him over the River Styx
into the windings of Lethe

Forgetfulness only for a moment

as the Bardos lift half a continent
and all the stages of death thru life
open in swirls of trajectory in
ceremonial caves out thru the mouths
the sweet fern breath flows cool
Halooo!   Haloooo!
and the Ego and interplanetary essences
combine
and dissolve

oh strict concordance
Terpsichore
an art that is constantly defying
gravity

~Leaps~

"an art that is constantly dying"
getting your body up into the air
to *fly   fly   fly*

62

on your feet on the floor
on stage forever more
I leaped
and wept
I *cried*
and stayed alive.
His world dominates this going by.
He "dwells with Beauty – Beauty that must die;
    And Joy, whose hand is ever at his lips
Bidding adieu; and aching Pleasure nigh,
    Turning to poison while the bee-mouth sips..."

Fly on Keats, fly on Keats, fly on.

His show, his hour before, on, and after.
It's going by, that is a memory roll
a light-fused spot light on full dancing stage
a stage gone by him he
them her – all achieved – on it
rotating, going, glowing –
by the applause and after it
that exact funny that, exacts in time
where was it that mind-space inhabits
bodies moved toward beauty, drawn
practiced by it, is, was it

    fly on, in and out
    on, in and out
    by for so long it
    went by.

High by for so long it went by.

/Sep-Oct87

63

GARDEN ART

Meredith Monk on the CD, turkeys gobbling outside
What is the reason for sickness, what is the reason for suicide
We might as well be pregnant with Spring and Earth-care
    anyway we can
and aim to turn this stage into a garden of new voices,
swelling wombs of paradise –
that is the ornamental grasses I plant in that corner
music coming up foreign to the jaded ear over there
until the artists with the freshest upstarts are planting rows
of the oldest plants known to agriculture reaches sepulchers of seeds
this momentary stage shines off eggplants,
pumpkin, new music, hybrids that will knock your socks off
what is the difference between plants and animals anyway,
we're all in this boom-boom together,
give everything we can to something new coming up.

/28Jan88 written for and premiered at *We Danced We Did* tribute
to Lee Connor, 29th & 30th January, 1988

The Center for Contemporary Arts of Santa Fe and
The House Foundation for the Arts, Inc.
present

MEREDITH MONK

SONGS FROM THE HILL (1977)
Music for Unaccompanied Voice
Composed and performed by Meredith Monk

1. Porch
2. Mesa
3. Jade
4. Wa-lie-oh
5. Insect
6. Descending
7. Silo
8. Breath Song
9. Bird Code
10. Lullaby #4
11. Prairie Ghost
12. Jew's Harp

INTERMISSION

MUSIC FOR VOICE AND PIANO (1972-1984)
Composed and performed by Meredith Monk

1. GOTHAM LULLABY
2. TRAVELLING
3. THE TALE
4. BIOGRAPHY

All compositions © Meredith Monk (ASCAP)
Lighting Design: Tony Giovannetti
Technical Director: David Moodey

SONGS FROM THE HILL was composed in Placitas, New Mexico in the summers of 1975, 1976 and1977. As in all of Meredith Monk's music, it is an exploration of the voice as an instrument, i.e. the full range of the voice (pitch, texture, volume, speed, timbre, breath, placement, strength): In SONGS FROM THE HILL each song deals with a particular vocal quality or character.

In her exploration and extension of the expressive ranges of the voice Ms. Monk has developed an unusually complex and fascinating vocal language which *The New York Times* music critic John Rockwell describes as a "perfected vocal technique in which she emits an amazing variety of sounds rarely heard from a Western throat, full of wordless cries and moans, a lexicon of vocal coloration, glottal attacks and microtonal waverings that lie at the base of all musical cultures."

MEREDITH MONK is an internationally acclaimed composer, choreographer, singer, recording artist and director. A graduate of Sarah Lawrence College, Ms. Monk has created more than fifty music/theater/dance and film works since 1964. Among her major works are *Break* (1964), *16 Millimeter Earrings* (1966), *Juice*: a theater cantata (1969), *Vessel*: an opera epic (1971), *Our Lady of Late* (1972), *Education of the Girlchild* (1973),*The Travelogue Series (Paris/Chacon/Venice/Milan)* (1974-76) in collaboration with Ping Chong, *Quarry* (1976), *Recent Ruins* (1979), *Specimen Days* (1981), and *Turtle Dreams* (1983).

"SONGS FROM THE HILL was composed in Placitas New Mexico . . .

65

Arthur Armijo

July 13, 1960
-
August 8, 1993

DANCE ART
Written for and presented at Tribute to life of Arthur Armijo

Are
are
are
Arthur
art
Armijo
may hold
may hone
are
art
Arthur
Armijo
may ho
my ho
me ho
mo jo
arm
may
hold
ho
main
hold
me
hold

upward cycle grace lines leap lone
fire bird
80's bold
lizard snake worm dragon
guy on the street bold
power hour after hour
grace substantial body
face a natural dance up
grace a power in control lost into
natural saving grace of
dance substantial natural grace

what lift to see dance at its ace
its junior king is
king come to home town to bring
the fresh rite of spring the natural
way of fall into it
dances upward with the best
to bring us fresh new presents
from professional afar
New York trounce the boards
and leap, leap fly back
a joy in our mind's body
dancing not still but
always such a fresh
spring comes old-new
again our
art art
are not through
art hours and hours of
dancing through us
only to admire
learn live king
Arthur dances through   King Art
the nights in shining armor of are friend
the flesh turned to beauty in   Arthur
the movements of dance that   Armijo
never stand still great   may go
             may hold
             us up
             may go
             may hold
             us up
             Arthur blessing us
             with
             dance
             Armijo
             dance are
             dance art
             Arthur

             Armijo.
                /26Feb94

Eva Encinias Sandoval and Arthur Armijo -
rehearsal for Connor Tribute

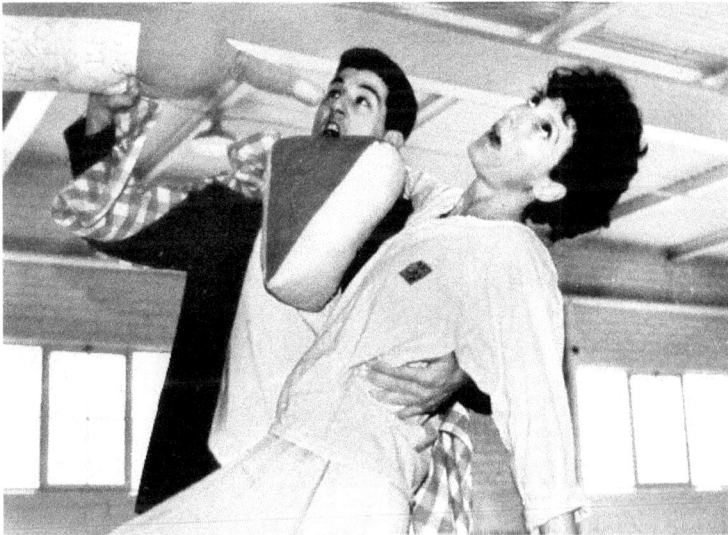

Arthur Armijo and Jennifer Predock in rehearsal for Connor
Tribute, "It's Either a Feast..."

Lorn MacDougal dancing in the tribute to Connor

Under It - Connor and MacDougal - Photograph by Lawrence Licht

IT'S ALL OVER, BUB

Ants in
pants ends.
Transcend
dance end.

/12Nov83

AFTERTHOUGHT

change evolves
in evolutionary change
chance change
change changes chance
it's all open, Bub
pull up your pants
get it going again
as it always will
new formations in the crack of Earth's
structure
and the whispering of the passing by
muse
muse of dance and every know creation
muse tickling
poetry in the ear.

/20Feb2015

DANZANTES, Inc.

presents

THE SEEING-IS-BELIEVING WISHFUL-THINKING
FOLLIES

with

LEE CONNOR
dance soloist/choreographer

and

LARRY GOODELL
poet

and

JEFFREY STOLET
pianist/composer

An evening of dance at crossroads with other
media, including collaborations with Barbara
Bock, sculptor; Jim Linnell, playwright; and
Jennifer Predock-Linnell, dance director.

Lighting designs bgy Karla Simmet

Kimo Theatre
Albuquerque, New Mexico

June 19 & 20, 1985
8 pm

73

HE WHO PAYS THE PIPER
CALLS THE TUNE

Lee Connor delivered this to begin his evening of dance.
Here it is in its entirety.

Good evening, ladies and gentlemen. Welcome to the
Seeing-is-Believing Wishful Thinking Follies. We have something kind
of special in store for you tonight. For your delectation and delight we
will attempt a feat which has been attempted over and over in theatre
ever since the less motivated among the Neanderthal decided to hunker
over there away from the fire a little, and watch their less sensible
neighbors continue making asses of themselves trying to become a
mastodon. This special tribe of mastodon-becomers has picked up quite
a few little tricks over the years. They have juggled and trilled,
pirouetted, orated, with uncountable refinements, and yet, after all this
time, not one of them, not one, has succeeded in becoming a mastodon
while anyone was watching. Some of us (and I count myself among the
humblest of this tribe, you understand) have turned out some fair
imitations, and along the way have accidentally or calculatedly
produced some nifty incidental effects, but capture the beast itself?.....
Never been done, as far as I know.

Doesn't stop me, though. Tonight, for the umpteenth time, I will try
again. I will, before your very eyes, attempt the contemptible. I will don
the furs of those voracious wolfish fiends that tyrannize the mastodon. I
will shake the rattle and tread tirelessly around the campfire. I will howl
the appropriate incantations and dredge up some arcane-looking
symbolic gestures, and the mood of the whole thing will be one of the
time-honored ones, a ritual self-disemboweling.

Oh, God! you say, this sounds like a major drag. How long is it 'til
intermission, dear? Well, don't jump to any conclusions yet. This may
turn out all right. I've given quite a bit of thought to trying to make this
as pleasant as possible for everybody concerned. I know I lured you here
with a fluffy, bubble-gum title and some other devious p-r ploys, but I
had to get you here to the Follies *somehow,* and I hope you'll forgive me
when all the wishful thinking you exert yourself to wish for, produces
nothing you can see worth believing.

Oh, God! you say again, when is this guy going to start dancing? Hey, buddy, raise that curtain, bring on the dancing girls! ...... Umm, this is *it,* folks. Whatcha sees is whatcha gets. This *is* the dance. The Beguine has begun.

...(dances a while)...

Yup, this is *it!* The 'Unhoped for Wave' in post-modern dance, *or* 'What Happens to Dance when It Stops Waving'. We all know what happens. Nobody notices. Dance has to be waving *something.* A red banner. A white flag. At least a pink hanky. You're probably pretty confused by now, and more than a little anxious. This isn't dance, you say, it just doesn't have any of the ... oh, I don't know what you call it.

Yes, you're right, in a sense. Most dances have clearer coordinate points for crystallizations of shape than this one does. But this is a unique dance. Unique because mostly it's an essay on what goes into a dance and why it registers an impact, why it does or doesn't elicit from you a full and appropriate response.

My problem is always, how do I get you to 'get' the piece? a) You have to see it. b) You have to commit to looking at it. c) Then, hopefully, you will really really see it. None of these steps is easy. First you have to be convinced that it's worth your while to come here. Against overwhelming odds, in spite of countless distractions and duties, you decide to attend, and you actually get here unscathed. Once here, you have to stay in your seat, and you have to stay awake. That accomplished, the chances of seeing the work (type "a" seeing) are pretty good. But in order to really, really see it (type "c") you have to look. You have to convince your eyebeams, already over-stimulated by a sensorially over-complex world, that they are thirsty for stimulation.

(While your eyebeams are warming up, we'll try to keep this dance on a fairly low level of visual stimulation. Gradually, when I feel you're ready for it, we'll step up the rpm's.) Oh, let up! you say. I'm ready already!

Okay, I know this is hard on you. You came expecting a nice evening out. Let Me try to get to the point. You are my patrons, and I'm very worried about our relationship. What do you want from me, what do I want from you, and are those two sets of wants at all reconcilable? Do I underestimate you if I worry you might not 'get' this? Do I underestimate myself if I suspect you have me figured out? Have you read into my dance all sorts of implications I never guessed at? You are so complex. I am so simple. All I ever wanted was to be loved, just obsessively and unconditionally loved, for trying to become a mastodon. Is that too much to ask?

Okay, you say. Shut up if you want to be loved! Dancers should be seen and not heard.

Well, let me tell you something. I've been poking around in the literature, as they say, and I've found out something I've always suspected. As soon as the mastodon-imitators began to want to spend the whole day perfecting their mastodon imitations while the rest of the tribe brought them hides and vittles, the tribes-people began to expect more and more from those nocturnal stampings at the campfire. Now this is not unreasonable. He who pays the piper calls the tune. I thought I'd share with you a few of the pokings-in-the-literature I found when I got interested in how things were for mastodon-lovers of an earlier generation.

Okay! Here we go! EXHIBIT 'A'.

To his Royal Highness, Monseigneur Cretien Louis, Margrave of Brandenburg.

Monseigneur,
As I had the honour of playing before Your Royal Highness a couple of years ago, and as I observed that You took some pleasure in the small talent that heaven has given me for music, and in taking leave of Your Royal Highness You honoured me with a command to send You some pieces of my composition, I now, according to Your gracious orders, take the liberty of presenting my very humble respect to Your Royal Highness, with the present concertos, which I have written for several instruments, humbly praying You not to judge their imperfection by the severity of the fine and delicate taste that every one knows You to have for music, but rather to consider benignly the profound respect and the very humble obedience to which they are meant to testify. For the rest, Monseigneur, I very humbly beg Your Royal Highness to have the goodness to continue Your good graces towards me, and to be convinced that I have nothing so much at heart as the wish to be employed in matters

more worthy of You and Your service, for with zeal
unequaled
    Monseigneur,
        I am
Your Royal Highness's most humble and most obedient servant

I don't know how this strikes you, but it strikes me as pretty sad.
This guy seems to think he's really a nerd, at best a homely, insignificant
fish in a vast, fishy sea. And you know who was just speaking? Johann
Sebastian Bach! Almost incredible, isn't it? One of the crowning glories
of our race, from the very first mastodonites right down to today,
abasing himself because the man who might pay the piper had power
and sumptuous means at his disposal.
    (Incidentally, there is no record that Monseigneur ever had those
concertos played for him.)
    Moving along swiftly, here's another case. EXHIBIT 'B'.

                    Leiden, January, 1737
Monseigneur,
    I shed tears of joy on reading the letter of September 9th
with which your Royal Highness honored me; in it I
recognized a prince who will be certainty beloved by the
human race. In every way I am astonished: you think like
Trajan, you write like Pliny, and you use French like our best
writers. What difference there is between men! Louis XIV
was a great king, I respect his memory; but he did not speak
so humanely as you, Monseigneur, and did not express
himself in the same way. I have seen his letters; he could
spell his own language. Under your auspices Berlin will be
the Athens of Germany and perhaps of Europe. I confess I
shall think myself very unfortunate if I die before I have
seen the model of princes and the marvel of Germany.
    I would not flatter you, Monseigneur, it would be a
crime. It would be throwing a poisoned breath upon a
flower; I am incapable of it; it is my very heart which speaks
to your Royal Highness.
    On arriving at Amsterdam I found they had begun an
edition of my poor works. I shall have the honor to send you
the first copy. Meanwhile, I shall be so bold as to send your
Royal Highness a manuscript which I should only dare to
show to one so free from prejudices, so philosophic, so
indulgent as you are, and to a prince who among so many

homages deserves that of a boundless confidence. Some time will be needed to revise and to copy it and I shall send it by whatever way you desire.

Indispensable occupations and circumstances beyond my control forbid me to carry myself to your feet that homage I owe you. A time will come perhaps when I shall be more fortunate.

Were I not so interested in the happiness of mankind I should be sorry that you are destined to be a king. I could wish you a private man; I could wish that my soul might freely approach yours; but my wish must yield to the public good. Permit me, Monseigneur, to respect you more as a man than as a prince; permit that, among all your grandeurs, your soul should receive my first homage; and permit me to tell you once more what admiration and hope you give me.

In whatever corner of the world I end my life, be certain, Monseigneur, that I shall constantly wish you well, and in doing so wish the happiness of a nation. My heart will be among your subjects; your fame will ever be dear to me. I shall wish that you may always be like yourself and that other kings may be like you. I am with deep respect, your Royal Highness's most humble, etc.

This is an even sadder case. These artists really had it rough. This guy is in real conflict. Obviously, he doesn't really believe this crap. It is very clear that he has a very high opinion of himself. This was Voltaire, and he ended up having a major falling out with Frederick the Great, so all this kowtowing, which went on for a great many years, ultimately came to nothing at all.

It became a classic pattern, though. The mastodon man telling the chief what godlike power he has.

Just one more: EXHIBIT 'C' will put us on a little firmer footing.

My Lord
    I rec'd the honour of your Lordships letter acquainting me that I am to expect Lady Dartmouth's Picture at Bath, but it is not yet arrived – I shall be extremely willing to make any alterations your Lordship shall require, when Her ladyship comes to Bath for that purpose, as I cannot (without taking away the likeness) touch it unless from the Life.

I would not be thought by what I am going to observe that I am at all unwilling to do anything your Lordship requires to it or even to paint an entire new picture for the money I received for that, as I shall always take pleasure in doing anything for Lord Dartmouth, but I should fancy myself a great blockhead if I was capable of painting such a Likeness as I did of your Lordship, and not have sense enough to see why I did not give the same satisfaction in Lady Dartmouth's Picture; and I believe your Lordship will agree with me in this point, that next to being able to paint a tolerable Picture, is having judgment enough to see what is the matter with a bad one. I don't know if your Lordship remembers a few *impertinent* remarks of mine upon the ridiculous use of fancied Dresses in Portraits about the time that Lord North made us laugh in describing a *Family Piece* His Lordship had seen somewhere, but whether your Lordship's memory will reach this trifling circumstance or not, I will venture to say that had I painted Lady Dartmouth's Picture, dressed as her Ladyship goes, no fault (more than in my Painting in general) would have been found with it. Believe me, My Lord, 'tho I may appear conceited in saying it so confidently.

I never was far from the mark, but I was able before I pull'd the trigger to see the cause of my missing and nothing is so common with me as to give up my own sight in my Painting room rather than hazard giving offence to my best Customers. You see, my Lord, I can speak plainly when there is no danger of having my bones broke, and if your Lordship encourages my giving still a free opinion upon the matter, I will do it in another Line.

I am your Lordship's most obliged and obedient
humble servant
THO. GAINSBOROUGH
Bath April 8th 1771

Poor Gainsborough! Such a problem making the Earl happy with Lady Dartmouth's portrait. At least he didn't lose every shred of his integrity in pandering to the dubious artistic judgment of that loutish lord. Not one of these men is creatively free. Not Bach, not Voltaire, not Gainsborough. And we mastodon men are no freer today. The big boys aren't and neither is little old me.

I have a great wish to re-arrange the universe. I can see all manner of motion, random and profuse, and I want to pick and choose some of them, clean 'em up a little, make 'em bigger, and smaller, turn 'em around, inject 'em with weird looking energy and bizarre shapes. I want to use all that stuff, that profuse, unthoughtful chaos of actions, to show you something. I want to say, 'I feel it like *this*'.

But what if you feel it differently, or worse, what if you don't get it? What if I seem not to have given any significant form to the chaos? What if I seem to you to have only added to the random clutter of our world? Have I failed? Is it my responsibility to give the world shape? Can I presume to do that for you while I do it for myself?

Let's make a deal. Let's all just pretend, just for tonight, that we're all getting everything just the way we want it. Like any old happy family, let's sweep the dirt under the carpet. We won't talk about it any more, at least for a while. We'll all try to get through to the end and hope we're still on speaking terms by then.

'Cause I have some nice things planned. I've enjoyed preparing them for you so much that I hope your enjoyment in seeing them will be half as great. If so, my enjoyment will be twice as great as yours.

Lee Connor, Dancer and Choreographer

Photograph by Bob Voca

"Azteca Ballroom" 1977 MacDougal and Connor

Photograph by Lawrence Licht

Note: "Azteca Ballroom" in New Mexico, named after the rehearsal space used in Bernalillo became an iconic dance performed on stage many many places including Downtown Saturday Night, Albuquerque; Zocalo Theater, Bernalillo; 4th of July Celebration at the Firehouse, Placitas, New Mexico.

FOR LEE CONNOR 1947-1987

Your silent center
Centered us all
As we waited for your mind to leap
In a taut gesture
Of imagination.
Yet your tension was so often released
In laughter
On stage and in the funny
things cooked in your kitchen.
Always unique.
More than original,
outrageous in dress,
courageous in thought and action,
How could so much courage come
From so small a body?
So small,
So strong,
Such dignity,
And at the end you danced
The Magnificat
Flat on your back
As once your women danced
In swirling skirts
The baroque wonder
Of the Brandenburg concerti,
Expressing for all the world to see
Your absolute love of beauty in
        all its forms
Shining from the stage
And now glowing in memory,
Changing forever
The way we see the world.
Changing forever the world we see.

David A. Bennahum,
Clinical Associate Professor of Medicine

Menu" for dance event at the
Central Torta, Albuquerque
Richard Thompson

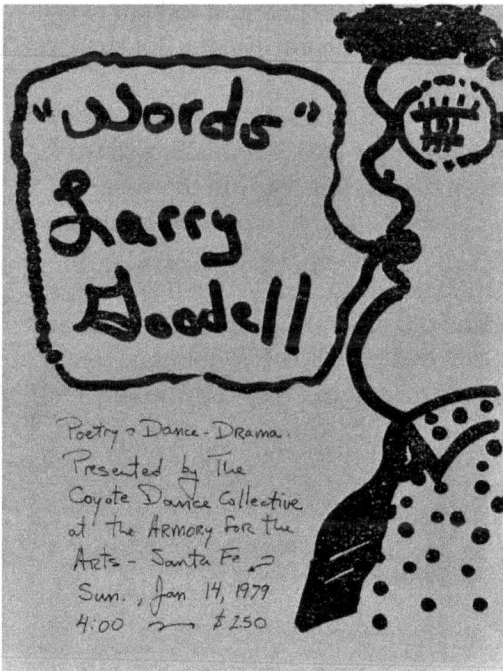

Richard Thompson flyer design for
collaboration with Coyote Dance
Collective - Stefa Zawerucha, David Fritz,
Frank Gilpin, Others . . .

ABOUT SUN IN THE MOUNTAIN

I have always been interested in the combination of forms of art. Large art. Extending from the page of the poem in and out of the ear onto the stage. Ultimately a *contemporary* opera, but that seems unlikely.

*

New interest in dance in Albuquerque makes it possible to work in cross-current art, that is, to me, each artist – in this case painter, poet, dancers and choreographers – contributing ideas, input to each other, as David & Stefa & Richard & I have done until coherent, separate contributions occur. We've met and talked and Richard Thompson did several sketches, drawings and then suddenly this poem SUN IN THE MOUNTAIN came to me and I wrote it down without any changes except for the very end which took a little work.

*

During the writing of the poem, and I do trust this poem, Richard's drawings began to run through my head and the presence of dancers took shape and at the end of the poem when the voice of the poet becomes the voice of his "inspiration" that voice says "Everything here is /Visualized there." So that everything going on on the stage – the set, the costumes, the dancers' individual and coherent movements – become the manifestation of the creative act. The *source* of creativity, at least for this particular performance, is revealed on stage.

*

So the poem begins with a kind of Rilke-like address to the source of all, *elan vital*, in this case kind of a male-female vibrating sense of Self that in a Upanishads way becomes all that is experienced in life. There is also a kind of Castaneda deserty primarily western-male presence. But the source the poet addresses is obviously All: "I step inside your door and we dance around the stove /In and out, you become the floor the walls the landscape/ The sunset, the wind."

*

The last two pages of the poem become the Source speaking, visually and vocally, and the sense of this being a winter solstice poem becomes clear, as all focuses on the dawn and the beginning of the Sun's journey back from the south. The Sun is vocalized as the Source.

/27Jan78 Mozart's Birthday

85

SUN IN THE MOUNTAIN

(First I speak to the source, using the words
of that source, more or less. Then, that source replies.)

I love your zigzag tomatoes and your profound courage.
You alone have led me through life.
Your stupified airs, your grace through the night.
Your rounded devotion and mechanical haze.
You have given me stupified wisdom, profound mother nature
                              and Early Pick tomatoes.
Thank God for your race your constant sliding air.
Your leg holds up the piano and without you the door wouldn't shut.
I live for your face in the toilet, the organ that comes out of your ears.
Your bananas that flop around awkwardly and peel themselves
                              before your very eyes.
Thank God for your odd head and your tomato warm bands.
You lead us through the valley of the moment's shadow of death
and you stop rolling, pop open and appear like crazy.
Thousands of onions are praying to you for their juices,
and get them, and eat them, and are eaten in turn.
Your table sliding warmth, attraction and fire.
Your devotion that splits open garlic and lets my hand in.
Your pickling pride, your tractor-riding power.
Your gift with little children as you give them toasters
and tie their cords up in knots.
You suffer the little snots up your nose and pass out playthings
and round handkerchiefs as every laugh is followed with a smile.

You are the hymn to the universe singing it as you go
down pathways and byways, down gourds and gorges
Up the fine highway to the dawn.
You are God, Don Juan, my uncle, our rocker with the back burst out.
You are rocking and rocking and lead us out of canyons
as ping-pong balls knock against the walls,
our sons hand us grapes and our daughters eat them
and our aunts are crying out the blues and reading leaves in tea cups.
I write as fast as my lips will move to disclose your face
your mind, your body, your secret inner parts
your Mondays, your blues, your ups downs sideways
your footballs and hair, your creature my design.
your mirror that leads me on
seeing future in my past
clearing up the hurts   cleansing the lungs
billowing out your directives like a giant wind,
your tendrils still clinging to the fence now in winter
when we wonder if the sun is going by-by
and if our lunacy is slowly taking over
and why each act we do seems entirely mad or a waste.
You are the billboard on my theater marque
revealing the oldest spectacle of all played backwards
and set right in the mirror you hand me.
You are the organ playing yourself endlessly
the chair I sit on which is blue, is stuffed, is spotted
and is labeled Stow and Davis Furniture Company.

Thank you for holding up the light when I fell down.
Thank you for dancing with me every dance a dying into
      the other.
Thank you for coming hack to life, Pete.
Sarah was expecting you and so was Sam.
Your oblong garage will park any car.
Only you can shake yourself free of dribbles when you pee.
The way your feminine curves are so beguiling.
Your voice surrounds the cactus bushes
pulls them up by the roots and plants them by the fence.
Your ruby lips come off revealing god-lines behind,
little cross patches with holes in them
fried in donut makers and served for breakfast.
I eat you with cream and throw the tofu out.
I change my manners and point out bad art wherever it exists.
I become the creature of darkness leading the lame.
I step inside your door and we dance around the stove
in and out you become the floor the walls the landscape
the sunset, the wind.
You pig out at the feast and I do too.
Oh graceful contours of all the veggies in the world
and some that aren't so graceful.
You and I exchange our plates and eat the same food.
You lift us when we rise and push us down when we fall
and without you the world would be absent.

You are the eye in the cup, the voice on the mesa,
the tadpole in the sink.
You divide us up into religions
and tear our hearts from our chests.
We become you because we come back to life.

We spread ourselves thin and work hard for a living
make crazy things, beautiful things sometime.
We go to counselors and listen to your sound advice.
Take heed! Take heed! you say.
Listen to my prayer, I pray through your lips endlessly
and clamp them shut
and listen to clouds.
          "Have you ever looked at a river?"
I listen intently.
          "Have you ever shined your car."
I screw up my brows.
          "Your breath would knock a bank off."
I shut my mouth.
          "Your navel has hairs in it."
I look down intently.
          The salt in the cup will make you see things backwards
          from the inside out.
          I am your alter, outer equal, your alter equal.

Spread your fine cloth over the high table and
lay me out on it. Take my cock in your mouth and play with it.
Caress my breasts.
Hold me, your best friend, in your arms.
When we embrace I am your best friend and lover
no matter who it happens to be.
I am the most equal human being you have seen,
through sex even the human body is beautiful.
Look at me on your altar, prepare the best food
from the best gardens you have.
          Even the human body!

Even sex can be beautiful through the human body.
The human body collapses and fails and then I enter it
constantly renewing
a bionic shot in the arm erecting your desires
until all hums and hums with fuzz
and stretching beyond the boundaries into waves of passion
releasing slowly the forbidden pleasure.

The stone in the cup looks up and is an eye.
I am the bird, the bird woman, the bird woman man –
I am entirely man to a man, entirely woman to a woman.
I am a surrealist pigeon, a parrot in a greenhouse of succulents.
Watch me come up. I am the bird leading the poet through
    the darkest days.
Now you are the poet being led, you have entered
the mind of the poet.
      Everything here is
visualized there.
You have entered and are me, leading you.
I have given you my gift of the poet
just what he can give, who is you now
to be that and whatever else you always are.
Watch me come up, leading and following
the distinct pleasure of words as they are given
distinctively, watch me come up, watch me
creatively   and without thought   clear as the mind
watch the sun come up.

              /18Dec77

design by Richard Thompson for dance - poetry
collaboration, Coyote Dance Collective in Santa Fe

dance flyer of CDC by Richard Thompson

David Fritz (1949-2014)

Note: David was a dear friend, close neighbor in Placitas, an enthusiast of dance. Working with David and Stefa Zawerucha and the Coyote Dance Collective was such a pleasure!

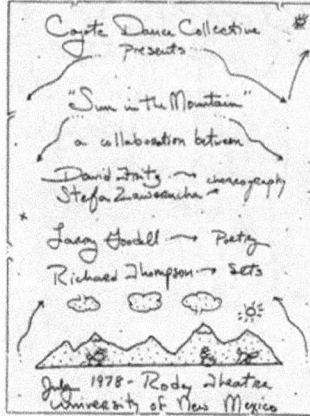

This collection of memorabilia and poems
is dependent on
the generosity of dancers and professionals whose images
are here to be enjoyed evocative of a remarkable time in Albuquerque
and New Mexico when dance simply took
off and ascended from the tarmac. I welcome any
corrections, additions, suggestions since this chapter
of living theater of movement and music
and poetry can only be added to
and improved
Thank you!
larry goodell

Marjorie Neset exerted energetic welcoming of exciting dance groups
to perform in the historic Kimo Theater in Albuquerque.
These and many more plus the Danzantes
boldly danced in Albuquerque
in the 80's.

SUSAN MARSHALL
A N D   C O M P A N Y

Choreography by Susan Marshall

Lighting Design by Mitchell Bogard

Dancers:

Arthur Armijo
Andrew Boynton
David Dorfman
Jackie Goodrich
Jeff Lepore
Susan Marshall
Eileen Thomas

Rodey Theatre, University of New Mexico
January 31 and February 1, 1989

The Foundation for Dance Promotion
in association with
The KiMo Theatre
present

BILL T. JONES/ARNIE ZANE & CO.
with

Bill T. Jones
Demian Acquavella   Arthur Aviles   Sean Curran
Lawrence Goldhuber   Gregg Hubbard   Heidi Latsky
Janet Lilly   Bunty Matthias   Betsy McCracken

Akiko Ko, guest artist

Artistic Director	Executive Director
Bill T. Jones	Vileana J. Briggs

Lighting Designer
Robert Weirzel

Production Stage Manager	Production Assistant
Gregory Bain	Monica Burrell

Rehearsal Directors
Sean Curran
Janet Lilly

KiMo

INVITATION
TO A COLLABORATION

MARGARETJENKINS
DANCE COMPANY

MARCH 20 and 21, 1987

KiMo

MARK MORRIS DANCE GROUP

RUTH DAVIDSON   TINA FEHLANDT   SUSAN HADLEY
PENNY HUTCHINSON   DAVID LANDIS   JON MENSINGER
MARK MORRIS   DONALD MOUTON   GUILLERMO RESTO . KEITH SABADO
JENNIFER THIENES   PIER VOULKOS   TERI WEKSLER

MARK MORRIS
Artistic Director

BARRY ALTERMAN	NANCY UMANOFF
General Manager	Managing Director

PHIL SANDSTROM	JOHN VADINO	ALBERT C. MATHERS
Lighting Designer	Technical Director	Stage Manager

93

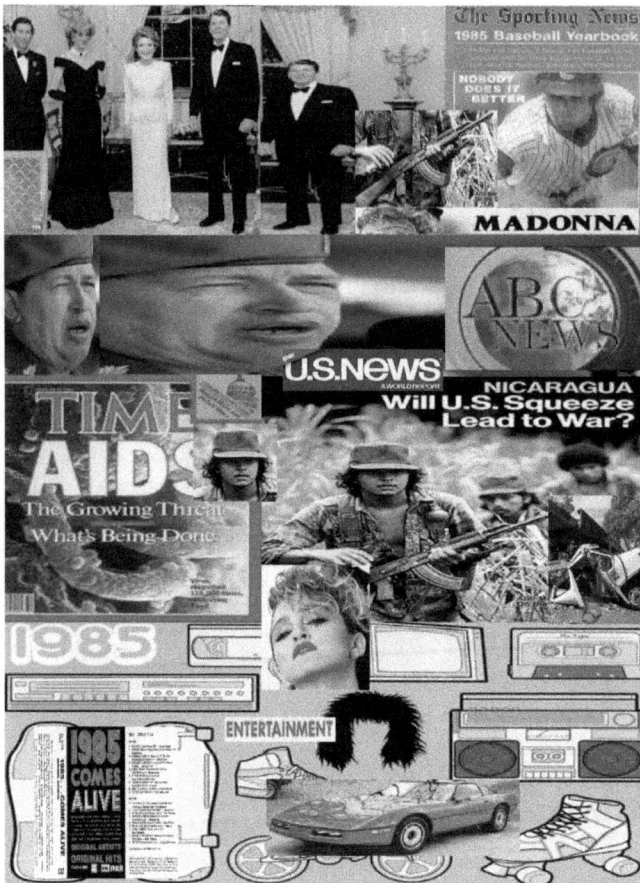

"N.E.W.S."

Dance collaboration between Lindsay Mayo's Dance Company and Larry Goodell produced "The News." Poem is Here:
https://www.scribd.com/document/628393128
/The-N-E-W-S-for-Dancers

ALIEN DOING
THE ALIEN DANCE

Love to All!

BY THE AUTHOR

Between Ann and Larry - letters Ann Quin & Larry Goodell
   duende 2023.
Breath - 2000-2002 poems, duende press 2021.
Escape - 2003-2007 poems; *Grounded* - 2008-2010 poems;
Commons - 2017-2019 poems, duende press 2020.

Hot Art and Other Plays; *A New Land and Other Writings*
   (prose), duende press 2019.

Nothing To Laugh About - 2015-2016 poems, Beatlick Press 2018.

Pieces of Heart - 2014 poems; *Digital Remains* - 2013 poems;
Broken Garden & The Unsaid Sings - 2011-2012 poems, Beatlick
   Press 2015.

3 dimensional poetry https://larrygoodell.blogspot.com/
lotsa larry goodell https://larrygoodell.wordpress.com/
duende.bandcamp.com for recordings / @larrygoodell

The Larry Goodell / Duende Archive is at the Beinecke Rare Book
& Manuscript Library. "It is a unique record of the thriving poetry
and small press cultures of the Southwest (and New Mexico in
particular)." Steve Clay, Granary Books.

DUENDE PRESS
the original   established in 1964
placitas, new mexico usa
larrynewmex@gmail.com   larrygoodell.com

www.ingramcontent.com/pod-product-compliance
Lightning Source LLC
Chambersburg PA
CBHW062005040426
42447CB00010B/1925